SPIKE
MILLIGAN

GUNNER MILLIGAN,
954024

D0306318

PENGUIN BOOKS

PENGUIN BOOKS

Published by the Penguin Group. Penguin Books Ltd, 27 Wrights Lane, London w8 5TZ, England. Penguin Books USA Inc., 375 Hudson Street, New York, New York 10014, USA. Penguin Books Australia Ltd, Ringwood, Victoria, Australia. Penguin Books Canada Ltd, 10 Alcorn Avenue, Toronto, Ontario, Canada M4V 3B2. Penguin Books (NZ) Ltd, 182–190 Wairau Road, Auckland 10, New Zealand · Penguin Books Ltd, Registered Offices: Harmondsworth, Middlesex, England · The full text of *Adolf Hitler: My Part in His Downfall* was first published by Penguin Books in 1971. This extract from that volume is taken from *Milligan's War: The Selected War Memoirs of Spike Milligan*, published by Penguin Books in 1989. This edition published 1995 · Copyright © Spike Milligan Productions, 1971, 1988. All rights reserved · Typeset by Datix International Limited, Bungay, Suffolk. Printed in England by Clays Ltd, St Ives plc · Except in the United States of America, this book is sold subject to the condition that it shall not, by way of trade or otherwise, be lent, re-sold, hired out, or otherwise circulated without the publisher's prior consent in any form of binding or cover other than that in which it is published and without a similar condition including this condition being imposed on the subsequent pur-chaser · 10 9 8 7 6 5 4 3 2

How It All Started

September 3rd, 1939. The last minutes of peace ticking away. Father and I were watching Mother digging our air-raid shelter. 'She's a great little woman,' said Father. 'And getting smaller all the time,' I added. Two minutes later, a man called Chamberlain who did Prime Minister impressions spoke on the wireless; he said, 'As from eleven o'clock we are at war with Germany.' (I loved the *we*.) 'War?' said Mother. 'It must have been something we said,' said Father. The people next door panicked, burnt their post office books and took in the washing.

Almost immediately came the mournful wail of the first air-raid warning. 'Is that you dear?' said Mother. 'It's a Jewish funeral,' said Father. 'Quick! Put out the begging bowls.' It was in fact the Bata Shoe Factory lunch hooter. It caused chaos until it was changed. Uncle Willie, a pre-death mortician, who hadn't worked for years, started making small wooden mushrooms. He sent them to Air-Marshal Harris requesting they be dropped on Germany to prove that despite five days of war, British craftsmanship still flourished. They were returned with a note saying, 'Dropping wooden mushrooms during raids might cause unnecessary injury.' My brother Desmond too, seized with pre-pubic patriotism, drew pictures of fantastic war machines. He showed Father: 'Son,' he said, 'these inventions will be the salvation of England.' They wasted no time: carrying the portfolio of drawings in a string bag, they hurried to Whitehall by 74 tram. After several arguments and a scuffle, they were shown into the presence of a curious nose-manipulating colonel. He watched puzzled as Father laid out drawings of troop-carrying submarines, tank-carrying zeppelins and some of troops on rocket-propelled skates, all drawn on the backs of old dinner menus. 'Right,' said the colonel, 'I'll have the brown windsor, roast beef and two veg.' Father and son were then shown the door, the windows, and finally the street. My father objected. 'You fool! By rejecting these inventions you've put two years on the war.' 'Good,' said the colonel, 'I wasn't doing anything!' Father left. With head held high and feet held higher, he was thrown out.

I was no stranger to Military Life. Born in India on the regimental strength, the family on both sides had been gunners as far back as the Siege of Lucknow. Great-grandfather, Sergeant John Henry Kettleband, had been killed in the Indian Mutiny, by his wife; his last words were, 'Oh!' His father had died in a military hospital after being operated on for appendicitis by a drunken doctor. On the tombstone was carved –

R.I.P.

In memory of
Sgt. Thomas Kettleband.
954024731

Died of appendicitis
for his King & Country

Now apparently it was my turn.

One day an envelope marked OHMS fell on the mat. Time for my appendicitis, I thought.

'For Christ's sake don't open it,' said Uncle, prodding it with a stick. 'Last time I did, I ended up in Mesopotamia, chased by Turks waving pots of Vaseline and shouting, "Lawrence, we love you" in Ottoman.'

Father looked at his watch. 'Time for another advance,' he said and took one pace forward. Weeks went by, several more OHMS letters arrived, finally arriving at the rate of two a day stamped URGENT.

'The King must think a lot of you, Son, writing all these letters,' said Mother as she humped sacks of coal into the cellar. One Sunday, while Mother was repainting the house, as a treat, Father opened one of the envelopes. In it was a cunningly worded invitation to partake in World War II, starting at seven and sixpence a week, all found. 'Just fancy,' said Mother as she carried Father upstairs for his bath, 'of all the people in England, they've chosen you, it's a great honour, Son.' Laughingly I felled her with a right cross.

It was now three months since my call-up. To celebrate I hid under the bed dressed as Florence Nightingale. Next morning I received a card asking me to attend a medical at the Yorkshire Grey, Eltham. 'Son,' said Father, 'I think after all you better go, we're running out of disguises, in any case when they see you, they're bound to send you home.' The card said I was to report at 9.30 a.m. 'Please be prompt.' I arrived prompt at 9.30 and was seen promptly at 12.15. We were told to strip. This revealed a mass of pale youths with thin, white, hairy legs. A press photographer was stopped by the recruiting Sergeant. 'For Christ's sake, don't! If the public saw a photo of this lot they'd pack it in straight away.' I arrived in the presence of a grey-faced, bald doctor.

'How do you feel?' he said.

'All right,' I said.

'Do you feel fit?'

'No, I walked here.'

Grinning evilly, he wrote Grade 1 (One) in blood-red ink on my card. 'No black cap?' I said. 'It's at the laundry,' he replied.

The die was cast. It was a proud day for the Milligan family as I was taken from the house. 'I'm too young to go,' I screamed as Military Policemen dragged me from my pram, clutching a dummy. At Victoria Station the RTO gave me a travel warrant, a white feather and a picture of Hitler marked 'This is your enemy.' I searched every compartment, but he wasn't on the train. At 4.30, June 2nd, 1940, on a summer's day all mare's tails and blue sky we arrived at Bexhill-on-Sea, where I got off. It wasn't easy. The train didn't stop there.

I Join The Regiment

Lugging a suitcase tied with traditional knotted string, I made my way to Headquarters 56th Heavy Regiment Royal Artillery. Using sign language, they re-directed me to D Battery. They were stationed in a building called 'Worthingholm', an evacuated girls' school in Hastings Road. As I entered the drive, a thing of singular military ugliness took my eye. It was Battery Sergeant-Major 'Jumbo' Day. His hair was so shorn his neck seemed to go straight up the back of his hat, and his face was suffused red by years of drinking his way to promotion. 'Oi! Where yew goin? It ain't a girls' school no more.' 'Isn't it? Never mind, I'll join the Regiment instead,' I said.

He screwed up his eyes. 'You're not *Milligan*, are yew?'

'Actually I am.'

A beam of sadistic pleasure spread over his face.

'We've been waiting for yew!' he said, pushing me ahead of him with his stick. He drove me into what was D Battery Office. The walls once white were now thrice grey. From a peeling ceiling hung a forty watt bulb that when lit made the room darker. A Janker Wallah was giving the bare floor a stew-coloured hue by slopping a mop around, re-arranging the dirt. On the wall was a calendar with a naked tart advertising cigarettes. Below it was a newspaper cut-out of Neville Chamberlain grinning upwards. Fronting the fireplace 5 was a trestle table covered with a merry grey blanket. A pile of OHMS letters, all addressed to me, were tucked in the corner of the blotter. In the lid of a cardboard shoe-box was a collection of rubber bands, paper-clips, sealing-wax, string and a lead weight. My pulses raced! Here was the heart of a great fighting machine. Seated behind this mighty war organ was a middle-aged, pink, puffy-faced man in his early fifties wearing a uniform in its late seventies. Parts that had frayed had been trimmed with leather; these included cuffs, elbows, pockets, gaiters and all trailing edges; for this reason he was known as 'Leather Suitcase'. His maiden name was Major Startling-Grope. 'This is Gunner Milligan sir,' said the BSM. When they'd both finished laughing, the Major spoke.

'Whair hev yew been, and whai are yew wearing civilian clothes?'

'They wouldn't let me on the train naked sir.'

'I mean, whai aren't you in uniform?'

'I'm not at war with anybody sir.'

'Silence when you speak to an officer,' said BSM.

The Major, who was fiddling with a rubber band, slid it over his finger.

'Does this mean we're engaged, sir?'

'Silence!' said BSM.

'I suppose,' said Suitcase, 'you know you are three months late arriving?'

'I'll make up for it, sir, I'll fight nights as well!' All these attempts at friendly humour fell on stony ground. I was marched to a bare room by a Bombardier. He pointed to a floor board.

'You're trying to tell me something,' I said.

'Your bed, right?'

'Right.'

'Right, *Bombardier*!'

'I'm a bombardier already?'

'Oh, cheeky bastard, eh? Got the very job for yew.' He gave me a scrubbing-brush with two bristles, showed me a three-acre cook-house floor and pointed down; he was still trying to tell me something. Leering over all this was the dwarf-like Battery Cook, Bombardier Nash, who looked like Quasimodo with the hump reversed. He was doing things to sausages. Three hours' scrubbing, and the knees in my trousers went through. To make matters worse there were no uniforms in the 'Q' stores. I cut a racy figure on guard, dark-blue trousers gone at the knee, powder-blue double-breasted chalk-stripe jacket, lemon shirt and white tie, all set off with steel helmet, boots and gaiters. It wasn't easy.

'Halt! Who goes there?' I'd challenge. When they saw me the answer was, 'Piss off.' I had to be taken off guard duties. In time I got a uniform. It made no difference.

'Halt, who goes there?'

'Piss off.'

Words can't describe the wretched appearance of a soldier in a new battle-dress. Size had nothing to do with it. You wore what you got. Some soldiers never left barracks for fear of being seen. Others spent most of their time hiding behind trees. The garments were impregnated with an anti-gas agent that reeked like dead camels, and a water-proofing chemical that gave you false pregnancy and nausea. The smell of newly kitted rookies could only be likened to an open Hindu sewerage works on a hot summer night by Delius. To try and 'cure' my BO I salted it and hung it outside in thunderstorms, I took it for walks, I hit it, in desperation I sprayed it with eau-de-Cologne, it made little difference, except once a sailor followed me home. Overcoats were a huge, shapeless dead loss. If you wanted alterations, you took it to a garage. But the most difficult part of Army Life was the 0600 hours awakening. In films this was done by a smart bugler who, silhouetted against the dawn with the Union Jack flying, blew reveille. Not so our 'Badgey',* who stayed in bed, pushed the door open with his foot, blew reveille, then went back to sleep.

* Badgey: Bugler.

Life in Bexhill 1940–41

In Bexhill life carried on. We went on route marches which became pleasant country walks. No matter what season, the Sussex countryside was always a pleasure. But the summer of 1941 was a delight. The late lambs on spring-heel legs danced their happiness. Hot, immobile cows chewed sweet cud under the leaf-choked limbs of June oaks that were young 500 years past. The musk of bramble and blackberry hedges, with purple-black fruit offering themselves to passing hands, poppies, red, red, red, tracking the sun with open-throated petals, birds bickering aloft, bibulous to the sun. White fleecy clouds passing high, changing shapes as if uncertain of what they were. To break for a smoke, to lie in that beckoning grass and watch cabbage white butterflies dancing on the wind. Everywhere was saying bethankit. It was hop picking time. In 1941 the pickers were real cockneys who, to the consternation of the ARP Wardens, lit bonfires at night and sang roistering songs under the stars. 'Right, fags out, fall in!' – of course, I almost forgot, the war! but people were saying it would all be over by Christmas. Good! that was in twelve weeks' time! I started to read the 'Situations Vacant' in the *Daily Telegraph*, and prematurely advertised, 'Gunner 954024, retired house-trained war hero, unexpectedly vacant. Can pull a piece of string and shout bang with confidence.'

I took my trumpet to war. I thought I'd earn spare cash by playing Fall In, Charge, Retreat, Lights Out, etc. I put a printed card on the Battery Notice Board, showing my scale of charges:

Fall In	1/6
Fall Out	1/–
Charge	1/9
Halt	£648
Retreat (Pianissimo)	4/–
Retreat (Fortissimo)	10/–
Lights Out	3/–
Lights Out played in private	4/–

While waiting for these commissions I'd lie on my palliasse and play tunes like, 'Body and Soul', 'Can't Get Started', 'Stardust'. It was with mixed feelings that I played something as exotic as 'You go to my Head' watching some hairy gunner cutting his toe-nails. Of course I soon contacted the Jazz addicts. I was introduced to six-foot-two dreamy-eyed Gunner Harry Edgington. A Londoner, he was an extraordinary man, with moral scruples that would have pleased Jesus. It was the start of a lifelong friendship. Harry played the piano. Self taught. He delighted me with some tunes he had composed. He couldn't read music, and favoured two

10

keys, F sharp and C sharp, both keys the terror of the jazz man: however, over the months I'd busk tunes with him in the NAAFI. I taught him the names of various chords and he was soon playing in keys that made life easier for me. He was game for a 'jam' any time. And of course, start to hum any tune and Harry would be in with the harmony, and spot on. It helped life a lot to have him around. One day, with nothing but money in mind, I suggested to Harry we try and form a band. Harry grinned and looked disbelieving. 'Just the two of us?'

'We could sit far apart,' I said.

A stroke of luck. A driver, Alf Fildes, was posted to us with suspected rabies and he played the guitar! All we needed was a drummer. We advertised in Part Two Orders. 'Wanted. House-trained Drummer. Academic Training advantage, but not essential. Apply The Gunners Milligan and Edgington. No coloureds but men with names like Duke Ellington given preference.' No one came forward. We were stuck, worse still we were stuck in the Army. But! Milligan had the eye of an eagle, the ear of a dog, and the brain of a newt (we've all got to eat). One meal time, as the dining hall rang to the grinding of teeth in gritty cabbage, came the sound of a rhythmic beat; it was a humble gunner hammering on a piece of Lease Lend bacon, trying to straighten it out for the kill. This was Driver Douglas Kidgell. Would he like to be our drummer? Yes. Good. Now, where to get the drums. Gunner Nick Carter said there was a 'certain' drum kit lying fallow under the stage of Old Town Church Hall. Captain Martin, a sort of commissioned Ned Kelly, suggested

11

we 'requisition' the 'certain' drum kit to prevent it falling into German hands. This sort of patriotism goes deep. With Germany poised to strike we couldn't waste time. We took the drums, and camouflaged them by painting on the Artillery Crest. Kidgell soon got the hang of the drums, and lo! We were a quartet!

After a month's practice, Captain Martin asked could we play for a dance. I told him we had a very limited repertoire, he said 'So have I, we'll hold the dance this Saturday.' GAD! this was the big time! Saturday, The Old Town Church Hall, Bexhill! who knows, next week Broadway! In entertainment-starved Bexhill, the dance was a sell-out. The old corrugated iron Hall was packed to suffocation; there were old women, kids, officers, gunners, various wives, very much a village dance affair.

After twenty minutes we had exhausted our repertoire, so we started again. I suppose playing 'Honeysuckle Rose' forty times must be some kind of record. The bar did roaring business, the barman being none other than the Reverend Clegg, Regimental Vicar. We played well on into the night. About two o'clock Captain Martin called a halt. They all stood to attention, we played 'God Save the King'. Now for the rewards. To pay us, Captain Martin led us into the Churchyard in pitch darkness. There he gave us a ten shilling note.

'A little something for you lads,' he said.

'Ten bob?' said Fildes painfully. 'Couldn't we raffle it?'

'Now then, lads, remember there's a war on,' said Martin pocketing the rest.

That night, by a flickering candle, we all swore allegiance to Karl Marx. No matter what, next dance, unless we got paid more, we'd play the bloody awful Warsaw Concerto!

Application for RAF Pilot

About now, of course, the heroes of the war were the RAF pilots. It made you green with envy on leave. All the beautiful birds went out with pilots. I couldn't stand it any more. I volunteered for the Air Force. I had to be interviewed by Leather Suitcase.

'I hear you want a transfer, Milligan.'

'Yes sir, I want to join the RAF.'

'Ah yes, those are the ones that fly.'

'Yes, sir, they go up, whereas we just go along.'

'Have you ever flown before?'

'No, sir, but I've been upstairs on a bus on my own.'

'No, what I said was, have you ever flown before? I didn't say anything about buses.'

'No, sir, I have never flown before.'

'Your father has written to me about it, and I will recommend you for a transfer.'

In February 1941 I was called for an interview to Kingsway House. I waited in a room with about forty other hopefuls. After an hour I was called before a man who appeared to be wearing a pair of hairy outstretched wings under his nose.

'I see you want to join the RAF.'

'Yes, sir. I have the character and temperament that is
admirably suited to that arm.'

'What would you like to be?'

'A pilot, sir.'

'Want to go out with pretty girls, eh?'

After a stringent physical examination they told me. 'Sorry, your eyesight isn't up to what we need for a pilot; however, we have a number of vacancies for rear gunners.'

'No, sir, I don't want to be at the back, I want to drive.'

'I'm sorry, lad, that's all we can offer you.'

I stood up, saluted smartly and exited. As I walked down the corridor to the street, I saw what was possibly the ugliest WAAF I had ever seen. 'Hello, cheeky,' she said as I passed her. Perhaps they were right, perhaps I had got bad eyesight. I caught an evening train back to Bexhill, and arrived to be informed by Edgington that he had read in the *Melody Maker* that Harry Parry, of the BBC Radio Rhythm Club, was holding auditions to find the best unknown jazz musicians – the winners were to make a recording for broadcasting on the BBC. We wrote off to Harry Parry, c/o BBC, London. We received a reply saying could we come down on the next weekend. We approached Leather Suitcase.

'You're going to do what?'

'Do an audition for the BBC.'

'You can't join them! They're civvies!'

I explained as best I could to him, bearing in mind that contemporary opinion of jazz in those days was almost the same as that of cannabis today. However, he let me go, and the following weekend, excited out of my mind, I arrived at the BBC Studios, Maida Vale. Briefly, I was picked as the best trumpet player, and along with the winning alto, 15 trombone and tenor players, we cut a disc. The pianist for this was the then almost unknown George Shearing, and for an hour, along with Harry Parry, we recorded six sides. It was an unforgettable day for me. I felt that I had been accepted as a jazz musician, and before I left, George Shearing said, 'I hope we meet and play again.' Man, that was praise enough.

Posting

Posting is an evil ritual: it was with devilish glee that one unit would pass on to another a soldier who they knew to be bloody useless. However, to keep the joke going, these failures were never discharged, just posted. There must have been, at one time, thousands of these idiots, all in a state of permanent transit, spending most of their life on lorries. Lots gave lorry numbers as a forwarding address. Hundreds spent the duration on board lorries, seven were even buried on them. There is a legend that the last of these idiots was discovered as late as 1949, living on the tail-board of a burnt-out ammunition lorry in a Wadi near Alamein. When located, he was naked, save for a vest and one sock: he said he was 'waiting to be posted'.

In 1941 a new power came on the scene. Montgomery! He was put in charge of Southern Command. He removed all the pink fat-faced, huntin', shootin' and fishin' chota-peg-swilling officers who were sittin' round waitin' to 'see off the Boche'. To date we'd done very little physical training. We had done a sort of half-hearted Knees-up Mother Brown for five minutes in the morning, followed by conducted coughing, but that's all.

One morning a chill of horror ran through the serried ranks. There in Part Two Orders were the words: 'At 0600 hours the Battery will assemble for a FIVE-MILE RUN!' Strong gunners fell fainting to the floor, some lay weeping on their beds. FIVE MILES? There was no such distance! FIVE MILES!?!? That wasn't a run, that was deportation! On that fateful dawn the duty Bombardier bade us rise: 'Wakey, wakey, hands off cocks, on socks.' The defenders of England rose, wraith-like, from their blankets. All silent, save those great lung-racking coughs that follow early-morning cigarettes. The cough would start in silence; first there was the great inhale, the smoke sucked deep down into the lungs, and held there while the victim started what was to be an agonized body spasm. The face would first turn sweaty-lemon, the shoulders hunched, the back humped like a Brahmin bull. The legs would bend, the hand grabbed the thighs to support the coming convulsion. The cough would start somewhere down in the shins, the eyes would be screwed tight to prevent being jettisoned from the head, the mouth gripped tight to preserve the teeth. Suddenly from afar comes a rumbling like a hundred early Victorian water-closets. Slowly the body would start to tremble and the bones to rattle. The first things to shake were the ankles, then up the shins travelled the shakes, and next the knees would revolve and turn jelliform; from there up the thighs to the stomach it came, now heading for the blackened lungs. This was the stage when a sound like a three ton garden roller being pulled over corrugated iron was heard approaching the heaving chest. Following this up the convulsed body was a colour pattern, from a delicate green at the ankles to layers of pinks, blue, varicose purple, and sweaty-red. As the cough rose up the inflated throat, the whole six colours were pushed up into the victim's face. It had now reached the inner mouth; the last line of defence, the cheeks, were blown out the size of football bladders. The climax was nigh! The whole body was now a purple shuddering mass! After several mammoth attempts to contain the cough, the mouth would finally explode open! Loose teeth would fly out, bits of breakfast, and a terrible rasping noise filled the room. Aweeioussheiough!!! Followed by a long, silent stream of spume-laden air: on and on it went until the whole body was drained of oxygen, the eyes were popping, and veins like vines standing out on the head, which was now down 'twixt knees. This atrophied pose held for seconds. Finally, with a dying attempt, fresh air was sucked back into the body, just in time to do it all over again. Bear in mind this was usually performed by some sixty men all at the same time. Whenever I see those bronzed 'Jet Set Men' whose passport to international smoking is a king-size, I can't help but recall those Bronchial Dawn Coughing Wrecks.

So to the great run. Hundreds of white shivering things were paraded outside Worthingholm. Officers out of uniform seemed stripped of all authority. Lieutenant Walker looked very like a bank clerk who couldn't. Now I, like many others, had no intention of running five miles, oh, no. We would hang behind, fade into the background, find a quiet haystack, wait for the return and rejoin them. Montgomery had thought of that. We were all put on three-ton trucks and driven FIVE MILES into the country and dropped. So it started. Some, already exhausted having to climb off the lorry, were begging for the *coup de grâce*. Off we went, Leather Suitcase in front: in ten seconds he was trailing at the back. 'Rest,' he cried, collapsing in a ditch. We rested five minutes and then he called, 'Right, follow me.' Ten seconds later he collapsed again. We left him expiring by the road.

Many tried to husband their energy by running on one leg. It was too cold to walk, we had to keep moving or hoar frost got at the appendages. One by one we arrived back at the billets, behind was a five mile train of broken men. It took two hours before the last of the stragglers arrived back. As a military disaster, the run was second only to Isandhlwana. It was the end of the line for Leather Suitcase.

Our new CO was Major Chater Jack, MC, DSO. In the

months that followed he ran us across two-thirds of Sussex, the whole of the South Coast, over mountains, through haystacks, along railway lines, up trees, down sewers, anywhere. If ever we had to retreat we were in tip top condition.

In the first week herds of men reported sick with sore feet. Busty Roberts told us the cure: 'Piss in yer boots, lads, let 'em stand overnight.' By God, it worked! There were accidents; forgetful sleepers got up and plunged their feet into boots full of cold urine. What an Army! What a life! I still can't believe it happened. But of course, the Russians were advancing on all fronts, the Yanks were coming, and we had our first case of crabs. I had no idea what the crabs (or, as Smudge Smith said, 'Sandy McNabs') were. The victim was Sergeant Cusak – he discovered he got them on the eve of a week's leave. The MO told him to apply 'blue unction'. Now blue unction has only one use – to destroy crabs. Knowing this, Sergeant Cusak entered Boots in Piccadilly with a prescription during the rush hour on Friday – it was crowded. He whispered to the assistant, 'Can I have some blue unction?' In a voice that could be heard up Regent Street the assistant said 'BLUE UNCTION??' Cusak replied twice as loud, 'YES, I'VE GOT BLOODY CRABS!'

Moving to Mill Wood

Nineteen-forty-one: during which the sole stratagem of the Army in England was one of continual movement. They chose the most excruciating moments. After spending months making your billet comfortable came the order 'Prepare to Move'. This time I was just about to lay my new Axminster when the order came. It was awful, I had to sell the piano. The moves were always highly secret and came in highly sealed envelopes, the contents of which usually appeared in later editions of the *Bexhill Observer*. Secrecy was impossible, enemy agents had only to follow the trail of illegitimate births. Another obsession was 'night occupation'. The swearing, the mighty oaths and clangs, told the whole area exactly what was happening. It was quite normal for a pub to empty out and give a hand pulling the gun. Most kids in Bexhill could dismantle one. Our first move was to a 'specially selected' muddy disused rubbish tip at Mill Wood, two miles from Worthingholm. The signal section under Sergeant Dawson had to start the lark of laying new lines. This was simple: you went from Point A, the OP and took the line to Point B, the Gun Position. Taking a rough bearing, we set off carrying great revolving iron drums of D5* telephone cable. We had to cross railway lines, roads, swamps, rivers,

* I don't know what it means either.

with no more than adhesive tape. We borrowed the equipment en route from houses, a ladder here, a pair of pliers there, a bit of string, a few hooks, a three course lunch, etc.

To cross roads we had to climb telegraph poles. Basically lazy, it took some half an hour of arguing and threats to get one of us to go up. It was always little Flash Gordon, he didn't want to climb the poles, but we hit him until he did.

We had a new addition to the family, a military ten line telephone exchange. This saved a great amount of cable laying; it also connected up to the GPO. It was installed in a concrete air-raid shelter at the back of Worthingholm. In 1962 I took a sentimental journey back to Bexhill. The shelter was overgrown with brambles; I pushed down the stairs and by the light of a match I saw the original telephone cables still in place on the wall where the exchange used to be. There was still a label on one. In faded lettering it said, 'Galley Hill OP' in my handwriting. The place was full of ghosts – I had to get out. One of the pleasures of Duty Signaller was listening to officers talking to their females. When we got a 'hot' conversation we plugged it straight through to all those poor lonely soldiers at their OPs and gun positions. It was good to have friends.

Burning of the Clubs (*Mill Wood*)

It was during this time the Goons in the Popeye cartoon appeared and tickled my sense of humour, and any soldier I thought was an idiot I called a Goon. This was taken up by those with a like sense of humour. We called ourselves the Clubbers. We built a club rack outside the marquee and, in time, we fashioned great gnarled clubs from fallen branches. They all had names – 'Nurkes Nut Nourisher', 'Instant Lumps'. The pride was a magnificent find by Gunner Devine; it was a part of a blasted oak, five feet long, almost a replica of the club of Hercules. We added to it by driving earthing irons into the head. It was solemnly christened, 'Ye Crust Modifier'. The way the Clubbers were assembled was by a trumpet call based on the Fanfare from the 'Boys from Syracuse' film. Immediately the gang would do 'Hollywood Rhubards', rush forth, grab the clubs, run into the woods hitting trees and shouting 'Death to the Goons'. This exercise was our downfall. We were caught one summer night by the duty officer. Drunk and naked, we were running through the woods wielding clubs and yelling 'Viva Joe Stalin'. We were ordered to destroy the weapons. We had a solemn funeral procession. They would have to burn in warriors' graves. These turned out to be the disused rubbish tip at the bottom of a gently sloping hill. Rubbish was dumped by trucks via a

small gauge railway. Filling the truck with clubs, we soaked them in petrol and set them ablaze. Giving the truck a start we jumped on, Edgington in front, holding on with his arms stretched backwards, looking like a ship's figurehead. The truck gathered momentum, flames built up, we were gathering speed and singing 'Round and round went the bloody great wheel', when suddenly it occurred to me there was no method of braking. As we careered towards a mountain of old tins, crying with laughter, I shouted, 'Jump for it.' We all leaped clear, save Edgington, who seemed transfixed. At the very last minute he let out a strangulated castrati scream and hurled himself sideways as the blazing truck buried itself into the mountain of tins with an ear-splitting crash.

It was a fitting Viking end for the Sacred Clubs. Occasions of insanity such as this stopped us all going mad.

As the days of 1940 came to an end, Dunkirk was sliding into history. The war was spreading; there seemed very little in the way of victories, there were constant reversals in Libya and Greece. On my birthday, April 16th, 1941, London had its worst raid yet. But cheering news – May 14th was the first anniversary of – wait for it – the Home Guard!

7.2 Guns And The Tiger Scheme

Our 9.2 guns were past it. Every time they fired, bits fell off. In place of bolts and nuts were bent nails and chicken wire. Gunners on leave would rummage through their sheds for screws, pinions, etc. The end came when elastic bands, which held the gun-sight together, were no longer obtainable. The Major wrote away, asking for a new gun for Christmas. One day they arrived. Dozens of them! 7.2 gun howitzers. Huge things towed behind Giant Schamell lorries.

At once we were put into vigorous training to familiarize us with the new toys. For weeks the area rang to the clang of breech-blocks, shouted orders, grunts of the sweating ammunition numbers. The guns threw a 280 pound projectile 17,800 yards, so you weren't safe anywhere except at 18,000 yards. Momentum was mounting, we were getting new field telephones, wireless trucks, wireless sets, tommy guns, Tannoy loudspeakers that linked Command Post to the guns. The war effort was moving into top gear.

Monty sprang a giant Southern Command scheme, code name 'Tiger'. One autumn dawn the sky was a mass of grey sponges: this undoubtedly would be the day. It was. Off we went. One hour after off we went we stopped wenting. We were in the middle of a Rain Forest that appeared to be in the Mato Grosso. 'Dismount' came the waterlogged order. Soggy officers were called to the OC's car. They stood in a squelching semi-circle, holding maps. Chater Jack whipped through the map references and all that Khaki Jazz. Our officer was Tony Goldsmith. 'We've got to set up an OP at Map Reference 8975–4564* in half an hour. Synchronize watches.' None of us had one. 'Very well,' said Goldsmith. '*I'll* synchronize watches.' Goldsmith's map reading left something to be desired, like someone to read it for him. Using his method, we had arrived at a hundred-year-old deserted chalk quarry. How can people be so heartless as to desert a hundred-year-old chalk quarry? We were two hundred feet below sea level. We got out. Goldsmith consulted his map. 'There must be something wrong,' he said, looking intelligent at two hundred feet below sea level. 'According to my calculations we should be on top of a hill, looking down a valley.'

Gunner Milligan said, 'But we aren't on top of a hill looking down a valley, are we sir?'

'No, we're not, Milligan. How shrewd of you to notice. This could mean promotion for you, or death. I suggest we retrace our steps to the main road. Does anybody know where it is?'

'I think I do, sir,' said Driver Wenham.

We boarded the truck, and set off somewhere. 'Send a message to HQ,' said Goldsmith, still trying to maintain the illusion of efficiency. 'Say, "Truck in ditch, will be late for OP."'

I sent off the message. But received a request for

---

* Somewhere on the South Downs.

Goldsmith to speak to 'Sunray' (code name for CO). What a lovely name I thought for a dripping wet CO.

Goldsmith spoke.

'Hello, Sunray, Seagull here. Over.'

Chater Jack: Tony? What the bloody hell's going on? Over.

Goldsmith: The truck's stuck, sir. Over.

Chater Jack: Well hurry up, the whole bloody battery's waiting for you.

We drove grimly on. One o'clock. 'Get the BBC news, Milligan,' said Goldsmith, 'you never know, it might be all over.' There were the opening bars of Beethoven's Fifth Symphony. 'I wonder if he gets royalties,' said Goldsmith. 'Oh yes,' I said, 'every Friday.' The news. Russians were advancing on all fronts. Then a list of current British disasters, retreats, sinkings, etc. The news concluded with a report of a two-headed calf born in Hereford.

Using all the skill of a trained Army driver, Wenham had the truck into a ditch a second time!

'Sorry, sir,' said Wenham, 'I won't do it again!'

'Don't stop now, man, you're just getting the hang of it,' said Goldsmith. 'Milligan! Send another message: "Truck now in second ditch."'

Back came Chater Jack.

Chater Jack: Good God, Tony, where are you man? Over.

Goldsmith: About a mile from the OP, sir. Over.

Chater Jack: You're very faint. Over.

Goldsmith: It's the food, sir. Over.

Chater Jack: I can't hear you. Look, we'll have to write you off. We'll get 18 Battery OP to fire us. Over.

Goldsmith: Roger, sir. Over.

Chater Jack: Anything else? Over.

Goldsmith: A two-headed calf has been born at Hereford, sir. Over.

Chater Jack: Two what? Over.

Goldsmith: Very good, sir, anything else?

Chater Jack: No. Roger and out.

We stopped at a village of Lower Lind, where we went to the Essoldo Bioscope Cinema to see *Dangerous Moonlight* with Anton Walbrook, and heard that bloody awful Warsaw Concerto. Lieutenant Goldsmith paid for us all, as is fitting for a man wearing the King's uniform over his Queens' College body.

He told me a story about Jesus College, Cambridge. It was Christmas morning. The phone rang in the gate porter's lodge. 'Hello,' said the porter.

'Is that Jesus?' asked a donnish voice.

'Yes.'

The voice sang, 'Happy birthday to you.'

At six o'clock we arrived at the night rendezvous, a field of bracken resting on a lake. We got tea from a swearing cookhouse crew, who took it in turns to say, 'Piss off,' to us. We were given to understand we could have a complete night's sleep. Good. We tossed for who was to sleep in the truck. I lost. Sod. Rain. Idea! Under the truck! Laid out ground sheet, rolled myself like a casserole in three blankets. I dropped into a deep sleep. I awoke to rain falling on me. The truck had gone. Everybody had gone. There had been a surprise call to action at 0200 hours. I was alone in a fifty-acre field. I shouted into the darkness, 'Anybody there?' I was still alone in a fifty-acre field. Smell of oil – I felt my face. It was smothered. The stuff had dripped from a leaky sump. Sound of motor bike approaching. 'Help,' I said. 'Who's that?' said a voice. It was Jordy Dawson.

'It's me, Sarge! Milligan.' A torch shone.

'What in Christ has happened to you?' he said.

'I'm doing Paul Robeson impressions. You're just in time for my encore.' I started to sing: 'Ole man ribber, dat ole . . .'

'What's that on your mush?'

'Oil, Sarge! I cut an artery and struck oil. We're rich, do you hear me. We can be married.'

He started to laugh. 'You silly bugger, we've had half the bloody signal section looking for you. The scheme's over.'

'I know! Half of it's over me,' I said.

'Come on, I'll take you back.'

'Go back?' I said in a pained voice, 'but I'm happy here, here on de ole plantation , massa baws.' Seated on the pillion, he drove me back to Bexhill. Tiger had been a roaring success. The German High Command must have been ecstatic. The following is an excerpt from the Regimental war diary of the time:

When the weather was too bad for schemes out of doors, wireless and telephone exercises were held within the Regiment to increase the proficiency in communications. It was on such an occasion as this, that a message was sent reading: 'Invasion Fleet in the Channel, two miles off SEAFORD steaming NW. Estimated strength three capital ships, sixteen destroyers, and many lesser craft.' He had omitted to prefix the message with the magic word 'PRACTICE' and by some unkind trick of fate, which has never since been accounted for, the message bypassed RHQ and was sent direct to Corps. The scheme finished, and the Regiment prepared to depart on its nightly occupations. Suddenly the peace was shattered by the frantic ringing of the telephone bell. It was a call from the War Office, who enquired, in no uncertain tones, what the thundering blazes was the meaning of our message. What steps had been taken by us: and had the Navy been informed?

By the time the matter had been sorted out, tempers were frayed and feeling was running high. It took some laughing off, but a personal visit by the CO to the War Office the following day succeeded in allaying the storm. It is an interview that few of us would have cared to undertake personally.

I think I can now safely reveal that the signal was sent by 954024, Gunner Milligan.

Things had been going too smoothly to continue as they were; it really was time we had another bout of applied chaos. It came in the shape of a sudden rush to Larkhill Artillery Camp, Salisbury, hard by Stonehenge. It was January 1942, and quite the bitterest weather I could remember. We arrived after a dawn-to-sunset trip by road. Salisbury Plain was blue-white with hoar-frost. I sat in the back of a Humber Radio Car, listening to any music I could pick up from the BBC and banging my feet to keep warm. We arrived tired, but being young and tired means you could go on all night! Ha! Having parked the vehicles, we were dismissed. The signallers were shown to a long wooden hut on brick piers. We dumped our kit on the beds, with the usual fight for the lower bunk, then made for the ORs' mess and began queueing. It must have been the season for schemes, as the whole place was swarming with gunners. We were given pale sausages, not long for this world, and potatoes so watery we drank them. The camp had masses of hot showers and we spent a pleasant hour under them, singing and enjoying the luxury of hot water. There were the usual comments about the size of one's 'wedding tackle': 'Cor, wot a beauty', or 'he's bloody well hung', or 'Christ, his poor wife', etc. After a quick tea and wad in the NAAFI we went to the large cinema Nissen hut. It was the Glenn Miller

Orchestra in *Sun Valley Serenade*, and it was a feast of great big band sound plus at least ten good songs. Sitting in the NAAFI later, we tried to recall them; it was this way that we learnt most of the tunes for the band's repertoire. Seated at the piano, Harry tried to play some of the tunes from the film.

'Play Warsaw Concerto,' said a drunk Scottish voice.

At dawn the next day the Battery set off on the great, ice-cold, frost-hardened Salisbury Plain. Most of us had put on two sets of woollen underwear, including the dreaded 'Long Johns'. We were to practise a new speedy method of bringing a twenty-five-pounder gun into action. Ahead of us would go a scouting OP; somewhere on the Plain four twenty-five pounders drawn by quads would be moving in the direction of a common map reference, all linked to the OP by wireless. Ahead the OP would establish itself at a point overlooking 'Crash Action East', or whichever compass point applied; the information was received by the gun wireless, whose operator would shout out to the gun officer the order received. The gun officer, standing up in his truck would shout to the gun crew, 'Halt, Action East'. The quad would brake sharply, the gun crew in a frenzy unlimber the gun, and face it east; while they were doing this the OP would rapidly send down the Rough Range of the Target. As soon as the gun crew had done this, they fired. In our case, from the first order to the firing of the first round was twenty-five seconds. This was the fastest time for the day.

The next ten days saw us going through rigorous training. The weather was bitterly cold. I saw Sid Price smoke a cigarette down to the stub, and burn the woollen mitten on his hand without feeling a thing. On the last day, B Subsection were firing smoke shells, when one got jammed in the breech. Sergeant Jordy Rowlands was in the process of removing the charge when it exploded in his hand. When the smoke cleared Rowlands was looking at the stump of his wrist with his right hand ten yards away on the ground. There was a stunned silence and then he said, 'Well, I'll be fooked.' Apart from initial shock he was OK, but for him the war was finished on Salisbury Plain. The severed hand was buried where it fell by Busty Roberts. As he dug a small hole Driver Watts said, 'You going to shake hands before you bury it?' Busty's reply was never recorded.

That night there was an Officers' and All-ranks' dance in the Drill Hall. We all worked hard to extricate all the best-looking ATS girls from the magnetic pull of the officers and sergeants. Alas, we failed, so we reverted to the time honoured sanctuary of the working man – drink. We finally reached the stage of inebriation when we were willing to do the last dance with any good-looking Lance-Bombardier. Next day, Saturday, the last day at Camp, we were allowed into Salisbury. I went to see the Cathedral. I'll never forget the feeling of awe when I walked in. A boys' choir was singing something that sounded like Monteverdi. The voices soared up to the fluted vaults as though on wings. The morning winter sun was driving through the stained-glass windows throwing colours on to the floor of the nave, the whole building was a psalm in stone. It all made me aware of the indescribable joy derived from beauty.

'Cor, it's bloody big, ain't it?' said Smudger Smith. He was right. It was bloody big.

There was a beer-up that night, and another dance. After 2343 hours I don't remember anything. Next day we returned to that jewel of the south coast, Bexhill.

Detention

October 1942. We were alerted for a practice shoot at Senny-bridge Camp in Wales. Burdened down with kit, I decided to hide my rifle in the rafters of the hay-loft. 'That's a good idea,' said patriotic Edgington. The short of it was several other patriots did the same. And it came to pass, that after we had gone thence, there cometh a Quarter Bloke, and in the goodness of his heart he did inspect ye hay-loft, and woe, he findeth rifles, and was sore distressed, whereupon he reporteth us to the Major, who on Oct. 14th, 1942, gaveth us fourteen bloody days' detention. For some reason all the other 'criminals' were sent to our RHQ at Cuckfield, but I was sent to Preston Barracks, Brighton, alone, no escort. Ahhhh, they trusted me. At Brighton station, I tried to thumb a lift; I got one from an ATS girl driving a General's Staff car. She dropped me right outside Preston barracks. As the car stopped, the sentry came to attention, then *I* got out. I reported to the sergeant I/C Guardroom. 'Welcome to Preston Barracks,' he said.

'You're welcome to it too,' I replied.

'Now,' he said, 'from now on you keep your mouth shut and your bowels open.'

Then he gave me a cup of tea that did both. He stripped me of all kit, leaving essentials like my body. The cell, my God! it must have been built in anticipation of Houdini.

36

Seven foot by six foot, by twenty foot high, stone floor, small window with one iron bar, up near the ceiling, wooden bed in the corner. The door was solid iron, two inches thick, with a small spy-hole for the guard. No light. 'You go to sleep when it gets dark, like all the good little birdies do,' said the sergeant. 'Make yourself comfortable,' he said, slamming the cell door. Every day, a visit from the orderly officer, a white consumptive lad who appeared to be training for death. 'Got everything you want?' he said. 'No, sir, I haven't got a Bentley.' I grinned to let him know it was a joke, that I was a cheery soul, and not down-hearted. It wasn't the way he saw it. He pointed to a photo of my girl by my bed. 'That will have to go,' he said.

'Yes, sir, where would you like it to go? I think it would go nice on the piano.'

'Put it out of sight.'

'But it's my fiancée, sir.'

'Photographs are *not allowed*.' He was starting to dribble.

'What about statues, sir?'

He lost his English 'cool'. 'Sergeant – put this man under arrest.'

'He's already under arrest, sir,' said Sarge.

'Well, give him extra fatigues for being impertinent!'

I planned revenge. I cut my finger-nails. On his next visit I placed them in a cigarette lid.

'What are those?'

'Finger-nails, sir.'

'Throw them away.'

'They are my fiancée's, sir.'

'Throw them away.'

'Very good, sir.'

The next time he visited I had cut a small lock of my hair, tied a small bow on it and placed it on my bed.

'What's that?'

'A lock of hair, sir.'

'Throw it away.'

'It's my fiancée's sir,' etc., etc.

The last one I planned was with an artificial limb, but the officer never visited me again. He was drafted overseas, and killed during an air raid on Tobruk; a NAAFI tea urn fell on his head.

My duties were not unpleasant.

1. Reveille 0600. Make tea for the Guard. Drink lots of tea.
2. Collect blackberries along the railway bank for Sergeants' Mess Tea.
3. In pouring rain, shovel two six-foot-high piles of coke into 'One Uniform Conical Heap'. (A Bad Day.)
4. Commissioned to draw a naked Varga Girl for Guard Room. (A Good Day.)
5. Trip to beach to collect winkles for Sergeants' Mess Tea.
6. Weed Parade Ground by hand. (Bloody Awful Day.)
7. Commissioned to draw Varga Girl for Sergeants' Mess. (Another Good Day.)
8. Oil all locks and hinges at Preston Barracks, sandpaper door of cell, prime, undercoat, and paint gunmetal black.
9. Drive Major Druce-Bangley to Eastbourne (his driver taken ill with an overdose of whisky) to have it off with his wife in house on seafront.

After fourteen days I was sent back to Hailsham – I arrived to find the whole Battery boarding lorries – yes! 'Prepare to move' again! With my kit I jumped into a fifteen hundredweight, making it a sixteen hundredweight.

'Where are we going?'

'I don't know, it's another secret destination,' said Sergeant Dawson.

Three hours later, we were back to square one. Bexhill.

'I wish they'd make their fucking minds up,' said Sergeant Dawson.

'Look, Sarge, they're moving us about to make us look a lot,' said Gunner Tome.

'We look a lot,' said Dawson, 'a lot of cunts.'

'Give us a merry song, Sarge,' I said, running for cover.

After the war, in 1968, I was appearing at the Royal Theatre, Brighton. I took a trip to Preston Barracks. All changed, the Old Guard Room with my cell had gone – everything had changed – except the large parade ground, that was still there; did I really weed it by hand in 1942? We must have all been bloody mad.

As the monkey-keeper at the Zoo said, when a new trussed-up gorilla arrived, 'It was bound to come.' We were going overseas. Of course we should have gone yesterday. Everything had to be packed into everything else yesterday. Somewhere great wooden crates appeared yesterday. 'Good God,' said Edgington yesterday, 'they're sending us by parcel post!' The crates were filled, nailed down and stencilled 'This Way Up' at all angles. Vehicles had to be waterproofed. Oh, dearie me! This smacked of a beach landing. Everything was camouflaged black and dark green so it couldn't be the desert. All our missing clothing was replaced. We then ran straight down to the town and sold it. One issue was a large vacuum-sealed tin of 'Emergency Chocolate', only to be eaten in the event of, say, being surrounded by the Enemy. That night, in bed, surrounded by the Enemy, I ate my Emergency Chocolate.

The news had been broken by the Old Man in the NAAFI hut, the dear old NAAFI hut. In it we wrote letters home, drank tea, played ping-pong, banged tunes out on the piano, or, when we had no money just sat there to keep warm. It was in this hut that I first heard the voice of Churchill on an old Brown Bakelite Ecko Radio. On the day of the official pronouncement, we were marched in and sat down. Enter Major Chater Jack, 'Eyes Front!' Chater Jack acknowledges Battery Sergeant-Major's salute. 'At ease Sergeant-Major.' At ease it is. 'You can all smoke,' said Chater Jack, 'I'm going to.' (Light laughter.) Smilingly, he starts to speak. 'You may have been hearing rumours that we were going abroad.' (Laughter. Rumours had been non-stop.) 'We are, finally, going overseas. It's what we've all been trained for, so, it shouldn't come as a shock.' He cut out all unnecessary gas and told us dates and times. A very Scots voice came from the back, 'Where are we going, sir?'

'Well, I know it's not Glasgow.' (Roar of laughter.) 'Embarkation leave will start immediately, married men first . . . they need it.' (Laughter.) A voice from the back, 'Don't we all.' (Loud laughter.) He told us that there would be a farewell dinner-dance at the Devonshire Arms. He finished 'Good luck to you all.'

I arrived at Victoria Station during the rush-hour. The crowds were a weird mixture of grey faces carrying early Christmas shopping. I was wearing my new red artillery forage cap, and felt rather conspicuous. I took the crowded Tube to London Bridge, and from there a train to Honor Oak Park. The faces of the commuters were tired and pinched. Occasionally one would steal a look at me. I don't know why. To break the boredom I suppose. A man of about fifty, in a dark suit and overcoat, leaned over and said, 'Would you like a cigarette?' 'Thank you,' I said, and like a bloody fool smoked it. A bloody fool because, dear reader, I had just gone through three weeks' agony, having given up the habit. As I walked from the station down Riseldine Road a raid was in progress. It was very, very dark, and I had to peer closely at several doors before I arrived at Number 50. The family were about to have dinner in the Anderson Shelter. 'Ah, son,' said my father, in that wonderful welcoming voice he had, 'you're just in time for the main course.' Holding a torch he showed me down the garden. 'Put that bloody light out,' said my brother in a mock ARP warden voice. The voice was in the process of breaking, and I swear in speaking that short sentence he went from Middle C to A above the stave. By the light of a hurricane lamp, called 'Storm Saviour Brand', I squeezed next to my mother. They had made the shelter as comfortable as possible, with duck boards and a carpet on top, an oil heater, books, and a battery radio. Mother said grace, then the four of us sat eating luke-warm powdered egg, dehydrated potatoes, Lease Lend carrots and wartime-strength tea. I felt awful. So far I hadn't suffered anything. Seeing the family in these miserable circumstances did raise a lump in my throat, but they seemed cheery enough. 'Got a surprise for you, son.' So saying, Father put his hand under the table and produced a bottle of Château La Tour 1934. 'It's at Shelter temperature,' he said. We drank a toast to the future. The next time the family would drink a toast together was to be ten years later.

Mother related how the week previously the whole family had nearly been killed. It was nine at night; Father, wearing aught but Marks and Spencer utility long underwear and tartan slippers, was heavily poised in the kitchen making a cup of tea, strength three. He was awaiting that jet of steam from the kettle that signals the invention of the steam engine. In the lounge, oblivious of the drama in the kitchen, were my mother and brother. This room had been modified into a bedroom-cum-sitting-room, double bed in one corner and the single for my brother in the other. This arrangement made my brother's night manipulations extremely difficult. However, Mother was seated on an elephantine imitation brown moquette couch with eased springs, knitting Balaclavas for the lads at the Front. My brother, Desmond, a lad of fourteen, was sitting on his bed, looking through his wartime scrap book, reading aloud sections on Hitler's promised invasion. A two-thirds slag, one-third coal fire smoked merrily in the grate. Suddenly, an explosion, arranged by Luftwaffe. Mother was blown six feet up in the sitting position, then backwards over the couch. My brother was shot up against the wall, reaching ceiling level before returning. The fire was sucked up the chimney, as were mother's C & A Mode slippers. The Cheesemans of Lewisham's imitation-velour curtains billowed in and the room was filled with ash. It was all over in a flash. My mother was upside-down behind the couch. My father appeared at the door. 'What's happening?' he said. He presented a strange figure, clutching a steaming kettle and smoke-blackened from head to foot. He said, 'Wait here,' went to the back door and shouted 'Anybody there?' He then returned and said, 'It's all right, he's gone.' Despite the activities of German bombers I was determined to sleep in my old bed. Sheets! Sheer bliss. Lying in bed I realized that the family was finally broken up – the war had made inroads on our peacetime relationship, I was independent, my brother no longer had my company. All was changed. For the better? We'll never know. We had been a very close-knit family, something not many British families were.

My week's leave was spent in 'sitting in' with local gig bands, seeing people from the Woolwich Arsenal (where I had worked before the war), drinking, and walking home bent double with sexual frustration from 45 Revelon Road, Brockley.

I arrived back off leave, and, I quote from my diary, 'Returned back at billets to find everybody drunk, jolly or partially out of their minds.' The knowledge that at last we were going overseas had given the Battery the libertine air of the last day at school. It was impossible to try and sleep. Everyone was hell-bent on playing practical jokes. Beds crashed down in the night, buckets of water were fixed over doors, boots were nailed to the floor, there were yells and screams as thunder-flashes exploded under unsuspecting victims' beds. The Battery was in a state of flux, most were on leave, others were about to go, others were on their way back, some couldn't get back, others didn't want to. One night the barracks were full, the next they were empty, God knows who was running us, certainly all the officers were on leave, what one good Fifth Columnist could have wrought at that time doesn't bear thinking about. I remember very well, one rainy night, Harry and I lay in bed, talking, smoking, unable to sleep with excitement.

'Let's go and have a jam in the NAAFI.'

It seemed a good idea. It was about one in the morning when we got in. For an hour we played. 'These Foolish Things', 'Room Five Hundred and Four', 'Serenade in Blue', 'Falling Leaves' and the inevitable Blues. In retrospect it wasn't a happy occasion, two young men, away from home, playing sentimental tunes in a pitch-black NAAFI. Oh, yesterday, leave me alone!

Friday, December 18th, 1942. The place? The Devonshire Arms. The occasion? the Farewell Dinner and Dance for D Battery. It was Chater Jack's idea, and I think I'm right in saying that he paid for the whole evening, because I overheard Captain Martin saying to him, 'You'll pay for this.' For the first time D Battery band didn't play, the music was provided by Jack Shawe and His Band. We would have liked to have played, but Chater Jack insisted that we had the 'night off' for once.

It was a marvellous evening. We all enjoyed the dinner despite the frugal wartime fare. The enthusiasm of the occasion was terrific. In retrospect I don't suppose many of the lads had ever been to a dinner-dance on this scale. It was the eve of what for most of us was the greatest adventure of our lives.

The dinner over, the dance got under way. Some lads had brought their wives down for the occasion, the local mistresses and girl friends were all present, everyone knew everyone else. I picked up with a WAAF Corporal, her name was Bette. I forget the surname. I ended up in bed with her, somewhere in Cooden Drive. I always remember a woman looking round the door and saying, 'Have you got enough blankets,' and I replied something like 'How dare you enter the King's bedchamber when he's discussing foreign policy?' This sudden late affair with Bette flowered rapidly and we did a lot of it in the last dying days prior to Embarkation. Actually, I was glad when we left, I couldn't have kept up this non-stop soldier-all-day–lover-all-night with only cups of tea in between. I was having giddy spells, even lying down. I don't suppose there's anything more exciting than a sudden affair; it is the sort of thing that defeats the weather, and gives you a chance to air your battle-dress. When I went overseas, Bette wrote sizzling letters that I auctioned to the Battery lechers.

The Train Journey (*Bexhill–Liverpool*)

The date was January 6th, 1943, the time just before midnight.
An army on the march. Weather, pissing down. Standing in a
black street, the hammer of the Germans stands silent in full
FSMO. With arms aching from typhus, typhoid and tetanus
injections, Edgington and I had been detailed to carry a
Porridge Container. 'Quick march!' Shuffle, shamble, slip,
shuffle, scrape. Nearing the station, a voice in the dark:
'Anybody remember to turn the gas off?'
   'Stop that talking.'
   'Bollocks!'
   'No swearing now, vicar!'
   The rain. It seemed to penetrate everything. We reached
the station soaked. My porridge-carrying arm was six inches
longer. Down the stairs we trooped on to the platform where
the train was now not waiting in the station. Permission to
smoke. An hour went by. We struck up a quiet chorus of
'Why are we waiting?', followed by outbreaks of bleating. At
2.14 a.m. the train arrived. Ironic cheers. All aboard! And
the fight for seats got under way. A compartment packed
with twelve fully-equipped gunners looks like those mountain-
ous piles of women's clothes at jumble sales. Once sat down,
you were stuck. If you wanted to put your hand in a pocket,
three men in the carriage had to get up. The train started. As
it pulled fretfully from the station, I suddenly realized that 47

some of us were being driven to our deaths! Edgington and I in the corridor decided to look for somewhere special to settle. The guard's van! It was empty save for officers' bed-rolls. Just the job. Removing our webbing, we lay like young khaki gods, rampant on a field of kitbags.

January 7th, at 2.45 that afternoon, we arrived at Liverpool Station. We detrained. Chaos. Non-commissioned officers kept running into each other shouting orders. Captains bounded up and down the platform like spring-heeled Jacks shouting, 'I say!'

Dawson clobbered Chalky White and self. 'You two! See the officers' baggage into the three-tonner.' Great! We didn't have to march. Gradually the Battery drained out of the station. We had to wait hours for the lorry. We loaded the officers' kit on, and drove through the black gloomy streets, with their grey wartime people, but it was still all adventure to us.

It was dark when we arrived at the docks, which bore scars of heavy bombing. Towards the New Brighton side of the Mersey, searchlights were dividing the sky. Our ship was HMTL15, in better days the SS *Otranto*. She'd been converted to an armed troopship with AA platforms fore and aft. Her gross was about 20,000 tons, I could be a couple of pounds out. Just to cheer us up she was painted black. Loading took all night; there were several other units embarking. We got the officers' bed-rolls into the cargo net, then boarded. A ship's bosun: 'What regiment?' he said, 'Artillery? Three decks down, H deck.' H deck was just above the water line, the portholes were sealed and blacked out, such a pity, I wanted to see the fishes. Along each side were tables and forms to accommodate twelve men at a time.

Fore and aft were ships' lockers with hammocks, strange things that some said we had to sleep in. Ridiculous! The lads were wandering freely, exploring the ship. Some had dodged ashore and were standing at the dock gate chatting up late birds. It was their last chance. Other more honourable men were furiously writing the last V-mail letter before sailing. I went on the top deck, aft, smoked a cigarette and watched reflections in the dark waters below. So far it had all been fun, but now we were off to the truth. I don't know why, but I started to cry. 11.30! There was to be a demonstration of how to live in a hammock. I arrived in time to see an able-bodied seaman deftly put one up between two hooks, then vault into it without falling out. It looked easy. Nobody wanted to sleep. I worked out we were waiting for the tide. About one o'clock the ship took on an air of departure. Gangways were removed. Hatches covered. Chains rattled. The ship started to vibrate as the engines came to life. Waters swirled. Tugs moved in. Donkey-engines rattled, hawsers were dropped from the bollards, and trailed like dead eels into the oil-tinted Mersey. We were away. Slowly we glided downstream. To the east we could hear the distant cough of ack-ack. The time was 1.10 a.m., January 8th, 1943. We were a mile downstream when the first bombs started to fall on the city. Ironically, a rosy glow tinged the sky, Liverpool was on fire. The lads came up on deck to see it. Away we went, further and further into the night, finally drizzle and darkness sent us below. I set about putting up my hammock. It was very easy and I vaulted in like an old salt. No, I didn't fall out. Sorry. In the dark, I smoked a cigarette, and thought . . . We were going to war. Would I survive? Would I be frightened? Could I survive a direct hit at point blank range by a German 88 mm? Could I really push a bayonet into a man's body – twist it – and pull it out? I mean what would the neighbours say?

On January 18th, 1943, I wrote in my diary: 'Arrived Algiers
at dawn.' Harry and I got up early to enjoy the sight of
Africa at first light. We saw it bathed in a translucent pre-
dawn purple aura. Seagulls had joined us again. A squadron
of American Lockheed Lightnings circled above. The coast
was like a wine-coloured sliver, all the while coming closer.
The visibility grew as the sun mounted the sky; there is no
light so full of hope as the dawn; amber, resin, copper lake,
brass green. One by one, they shed themselves until the sun
rose golden in a white sky. Lovely morning warmth. I closed
my eyes and turned my face to the sun. I fell down a
hatchway. 'Awake!' said Harry down the hole, 'for Morning
in the Bowl of Night, Has flung the Stone that puts the Stars
to flight. Omar Khayyam.' 'Get stuffed. Spike Milligan.' The
convoy was now in line ahead making for the port. Gradually
the buildings of Algiers grew close. The city was built on a
hill, and tiered, most buildings were white. We were closing
to the dockside. Activity. Khaki figures were swarming everywhere. Trucks, tanks, aircraft, guns, shells, all were being
off-loaded. Odd gendarmes looked helpless, occasionally
blew whistles, pointed at Arabs, then hit them. They'd lost
the war and by God they were going to take it out on
someone. Now we could see palm-tree-lined boulevards. We
made the last raid on the canteen, stocked up with fags,   51

chocolate and anything. In full FSMO (pronounced Effessm-mmoh) we paraded on deck. I tell you, each man had so much kit it reminded me of that bloody awful Warsaw Concerto. A bombardier came round and distributed little booklets saying: 'Customs and Habits of French North Africa. How to behave. The Currency. Addresses of Post-Brothel Military Clinics.' And a contraceptive. Only one? They must be expecting a short war. Harry Edgington was horrified. 'Look at this,' he said, his lovely face dark with rage, 'putting temptation in a man's hands.' Whereupon he hurled it overboard. Others blew them up and paddled them ashore shouting, 'Happy New Year.' Down came the gangplanks and the 56th Heavy Regiment, ten days at sea, heavier than it had ever had been, debouched.

We marched through the palm-lined streets, into a vast concrete football stadium. On the pitch were scores of tents. It must have been half-time, I thought. But no! They were the bivouacs of a Scots battalion, just back from the front. Hanging on the washing lines were battle-scarred kilts. It must have been hell under there! It was a vast concrete football stadium. I mention that again in the nature of an encore. All the action was around a field kitchen. Several queues all converged on one point where a cook, with a handle-bar moustache, and of all things a monocle, was doling out. He once had a glass eye that shot out when he sneezed and fell in the porridge so he wore the monocle as a sort of optical condom. He doled out something into my mess tin. 'What is it?' I asked. 'Irish stew,' he said. 'Then,' I replied, 'Irish stew in the name of the law.' It was a vast concrete arena. We queued for an hour. When that had passed we queued for blankets. Next, find somewhere to sleep, like a football stadium in North Africa. We dossed down on the terraces. After ship's hammocks it was murder. If only, if *only* I had a grand piano. I could have slept in that. Anything was better than a vast concrete arena. At dawn my frozen body signalled me, arise. I stamped around the freezing terraces to get warm. I lit up a fag and went scrounging. There were still a few embers burning in the field kitchen. I found a tea urn full of dead leaves from which I managed to get a fresh brew.

Gradually the sun came up. There was no way of stopping it. It rose from the east like an iridescent gold Napoleon. It filled the dawn sky with swathes of pink, orange and flame. Breakfast was bully beef and hard tack. I washed and shaved under a tap, icy cold, still, it was good for the complexion. 'Gunners! Stay lovely for your commanding officer with Algerian football stadium water!' I stood at the gates watching people in the streets. I made friends with two little French kids on their way to school, a girl and a boy. I gave them two English pennies. In exchange they gave me an empty matchbox, with a camel label on the top. I shall always remember their faces. A gentle voice behind me. 'Where the bleedin' 'ell you bin?' It was Jordy Dawson. 'Come on, we're off to the docks.' And so we were.

Arriving there we checked that all D Battery kitbags were on board our lorries, then drove off. The direction was east along the coast road to Jean Bart. We sat with our legs dangling over the tail-board. Whenever we passed French colonials, some of them gave us to understand that our presence in the Dark Continent was not wanted by a simple explicative gesture from the waist down. We passed through dusty scrub-like countryside with the sea to our left. In little batches we passed Arabs with camels or donkeys, children begging or selling tangerines and eggs. The cactus fruit was all ripe, pillar-box red. I hadn't seen any since I was a boy in India. The road curved gradually and the land gradient rose slightly and revealed to us a grand view of the Bay of Algiers. Rich blue, with morning sunshine tinselling the waves. Our driver, 'Hooter Price' (so called because of a magnificent large nose shaped like a pennant; when he swam on his back, people shouted, 'Sharks') was singing, 'I'll be seeing you,' as we jostled along the dusty road. It was twenty-six miles to our destination, with the mysterious name 'X Camp', situated just half a mile inland at Cap Matifou. X Camp was proving an embarrassment to Army Command. It was built to house German prisoners of war. Somehow we hadn't managed to get any, so, to give it the appearance of being a success, 56 Heavy Regiment were marched in and told that this was, for the time being, 'home'. When D Battery heard this, it was understandable when roll-call was made the first morning:

'Gunner Devine?'
'Ya wol!'
'Gunner Spencer?'
'Ya!'
'Gunner Maunders?'
'Ya wol!'

The march of the regiment from the ship to Cap Matifou had been a mild disaster. It started in good march style, but gradually, softened by two weeks at sea, and in full FSMO, two-thirds of the men gradually fell behind and finally everyone was going it alone at his own pace. A long string of men stretched over twenty-six miles. I quote from Major Chater Jack's recollection of the incident in a letter he wrote to me in 1957. 'Perhaps some will remember the landing at Algiers and that ghastly march with full kit, for which we were not prepared. The march ended after dark, somewhere beyond Maison Blanche, and was rather a hard initiation into war – a valuable initiation though, for it made many things thereafter seem easier!' To top it all there was a tragedy – Driver Reed, who flaked out on the march, tried to hop a lift but fell between the lorry and trailer and was squashed to death. The only way to unstick him from the road was by pulling at his webbing straps. Tragedy number two was Gunner Leigh, thirty-six (old for a soldier); as he arrived at the camp he received a telegram telling him his wife and three children had been killed in a raid on Liverpool. He went insane and never spoke again. He is still in a mental home near Menston in Yorkshire.

Sanitary Orderly Liddel was learning the trade of maintenance on the outdoor hole-in-the-ground latrines. The lime powder that is normally used to 'sprinkle' the pit had not arrived. He, being of an inventive turn of mind, mixed petrol and diesel and used that. Dawn! Enter an RSM, pleasure-bent! He squats on pole. Lights pipe, drops match. BOOOOOOOOM! There emerges smoke-blackened figure, trousers down, smouldering shirt tail, singed eyebrows, second-degree burns on bum – a sort of English loss of face.

He was our last casualty before we actually went into action. Next time it would be for real.

PENGUIN 60s

READ MORE IN PENGUIN

For complete information about books available from Penguin and how to order them, please write to us at the appropriate address below. Please note that for copyright reasons the selection of books varies from country to country.

IN THE UNITED KINGDOM: Please write to *Dept. JC, Penguin Books Ltd, FREEPOST, West Drayton, Middlesex UB7 0BR.*
If you have any difficulty in obtaining a title, please send your order with the correct money, plus ten per cent for postage and packaging, to *PO Box No. 11, West Drayton, Middlesex UB7 0BR.*

IN THE UNITED STATES: Please write to *Consumer Sales, Penguin USA, P.O. Box 999, Dept. 17109, Bergenfield, New Jersey 07621-0120.* VISA and MasterCard holders call 1-800-253-6476 to order all Penguin titles.

IN CANADA: Please write to *Penguin Books Canada Ltd, 10 Alcorn Avenue, Suite 300, Toronto, Ontario M4V 3B2.*

IN AUSTRALIA: Please write to *Penguin Books Australia Ltd, P.O. Box 257, Ringwood, Victoria 3134.*

IN NEW ZEALAND: Please write to *Penguin Books (NZ) Ltd, Private Bag 102902, North Shore Mail Centre, Auckland 10.*

IN INDIA: Please write to *Penguin Books India Pvt Ltd, 706 Eros Apartments, 56 Nehru Place, New Delhi 110 019.*

IN THE NETHERLANDS: Please write to *Penguin Books Netherlands bv, Postbus 3507, NL-1001 AH Amsterdam.*

IN GERMANY: Please write to *Penguin Books Deutschland GmbH, Metzlerstrasse 26, 60594 Frankfurt am Main.*

IN SPAIN: Please write to *Penguin Books S. A., Bravo Murillo 19, 1o B, 28015 Madrid.*

IN ITALY: Please write to *Penguin Italia s.r.l., Via Felice Casati 20, I-20124 Milano.*

IN FRANCE: Please write to *Penguin France S. A., 17 rue Lejeune, F-31000 Toulouse.*

IN JAPAN: Please write to *Penguin Books Japan, Ishikiribashi Building, 2-5-4, Suido, Bunkyo-ku, Tokyo 112.*

IN GREECE: Please write to *Penguin Hellas Ltd, Dimocritou 3, GR-106 71 Athens.*

IN SOUTH AFRICA: Please write to *Longman Penguin Southern Africa (Pty) Ltd, Private Bag X08, Bertsham 2013.*